When delicious happens to be Vegan

ON A VEGAN TABLE

Breakfast & Dessert Edition

by Lucille Molerus

When delicious happens to be Vegan

CONTENTS

Table of

MAIN INGREDIENTS

Active dry yeast: *As a leavening agent for breads and brioche buns.*

Apple sauce: *Used as an egg substitute to bring moisture and for the binding properties of the pectin. To make it cut apple into squares, place in a small saucepan, add a little water, cover, and cook for 10 minutes. Mix in the small food processor and let cool. If you use store bought, prefer sugar free.*

Cashew butter: *The smoother the better.*

Coconut oil: *Prefer refined coconut oil which is odorless, otherwise it would take over the other flavors.*

Flour: *All-purpose flour is used for all the recipes.*

Maple syrup: *Because it is the best.*

Oats: *Depending on the recipe any oats or quick oats.*

Olive oil: *Cold-pressed extra virgin olive oil.*

Pumpkin puree: *To add some color or as an egg substitute.*

Sugar: *Regular white sugar and brown sugar for some recipes.*

Vanilla extract: *Any vanilla extract.*

Vegan butter: *I use soft plant-based butter with 55% fat made with vegetable oils. If you live in the US, Trader Joe's vegan butter is really good.*

Appliances: *Digital kitchen scale, High speed blender, Stand mixer, Immersion blender, and Small food processor.*

ON A VEGAN TABLE - THE COOKBOOK

These recipes are not meant to be healthy, they are meant to be indulgent! Having had to become vegan for health reasons, food could not be yet another reminder of those issues. Therefore, I decided to change my perspective on what a plant-based diet looked like. I must admit I had a lot of preconceptions on vegan food and was pretty angry that butter was taken away from me. But after a lot of research and some pretty bad results, I finally found my ground and a way of fully satisfying my taste buds.

Now I am sharing my vision of plant-based food through my Instagram, my website, and this cookbook, hoping you will enjoy the recipes whether you are vegan or not, and maybe change a few minds on what eating vegan looks like!

All the breakfast and dessert recipes are simple and accessible for everyday baking.

The idea behind all my recipes is to not imitate non-vegan recipes because the results are usually disappointing and involve complicated ingredients. You will tell me, then why try to make vegan cinnamon buns? The answer is because you can! I didn't think it was possible at first, but it turns out the vegan version is even better than the original! And who wants to live in a world without warm cinnamon buns? Once you understand how to bake with plant-based ingredients, the results are delicious! Just as classic recipes have been perfected for decades, imagine all the recipes we will create by giving the same attention to new plant-based ingredients. An inspiring perspective!

Hope you enjoy.

BREAKFAST BREADS AND BRIOCHE

Fruits and Cashew Milk

Eating fruit as cereal with homemade cashew milk. It is made in a matter of minutes using cashew butter instead of whole cashews, specifically the hard cashew butter that sticks at the bottom of the jar that never gets used.

Makes	1 portion
Prep time	10 min

Cashew milk

25 g	**Cashew butter**
150 ml	**Water**
2 tsp	**Maple syrup**
Pincée	**Salt**

Fruits

150 g	**Strawberries**
1	**Peach**
100 g	**Blueberries**

For the cashew milk, use the creamiest cashew butter you can find. Mix all the ingredients in a small food processor for 30 seconds. Add more maple syrup for extra sweetness or a little cashew butter for a richer, creamier milk.

Wash and cut the fruits into bite size pieces. Three fruits is usually a good combination, more would be too many. This bowl is filled with strawberries, peaches, and blueberries.

Homemade Oat Milk

Oat milk is so quick and easy to make with a high-speed blender that it's really not worth buying it. The other upside is that you can make just the amount you need.

Makes   840 ml

Prep time 10 min

90 g   **Oats**

820 ml   **Water**

1 tbsp   **Maple syrup**

Pinch of   **Salt**

1 tsp   **Vanilla extract**
            (optionnal)

Blend all the ingredients in a high-speed blender for 20 to 30 seconds. Do not blend for too long otherwise it will develop the gelatinous properties of the oats.

Drain the mixture through a thin thieve, press it down to squeeze out all the milk. Keep the pulp to make other recipes and store the milk in the refrigerator in a mason jar or milk bottle for up to 3 days.

Use this milk to make brioche, tigelle, chia pudding, even crêpes or pour over homemade granola.

The oat pulp can be kept a couple of days in the refrigerator or frozen in ice cube trays to use later. Add it to overnight oats or use it to make the orange scones or apple cinnamon cake recipes.

Brioche

Brioche is traditional French soft bread made with an enriched dough. This vegan version is the fluffiest, lightest brioche ever. Before making this recipe make some potato yeast. Weird? I know, but it will make such a difference, giving the brioche a buttery taste and an incredibly light texture.

Prep time: 30 minutes, 3 hours or overnight in the refrigerator to proof, 30 minutes to shape, 1h30 to rise, and 25 minutes to bake

Makes 10 slices

210 ml	**Oat milk** (p. 14)
1 tsp	**Active dry yeast**
43 g	**Potato yeast** (p. 20)
80 g	**Vegan butter**
430 g	**Flour**
90 g	**Sugar**
½ tsp	**Salt**

The brioche can be kneaded by hand but that will take longer.

Heat the plant milk to lukewarm 30 seconds in the microwave. Whisk in the active dry yeast and the potato yeast. Let sit for 10 minutes to activate.

Melt the vegan butter 20 seconds in the microwave.

Prepare the dry ingredients: the flour, sugar, and salt. Roughly combine.

Pour the milk and yeast mixture in the bowl of a stand mixer*. Pass it through a fine sieve if there are any lumps left and press hard with the back of a spoon to get everything out. Add the vegan butter, then the dry ingredients and knead for 6 to 8 minutes with a stand mixer. Stop halfway to scrap down the sides if needed. The dough will not completely detach from the bowl to form a ball, that's fine, it just needs to be smooth.

Using a spatula, bring the dough towards the center to form a rough ball. Transfer it to a bowl with enough room for it to rise and cover with a lid or plastic wrap. Chill in the refrigerator at least 3 hours or, even better, overnight (up to 24h) to enhance the brioche flavor.

Lightly butter and flour a 11x4-inch (28 by 11 cm) loaf pan.

Take the dough out of the refrigerator.

On a lightly floured surface, roll it out into a rough rectangle. Fold it in 3, turn the dough a quarter of a circle and repeat this two more times. Roll it out into a rectangle of about 16 inches long (40 cm) and make 2 incisions lengthwise to divide it into 3 equal parts. Do not cut it on the entire length. Braid the dough and place it in the loaf pan. Cover with plastic wrap and place 1h30, or until it has doubled in size, in a warm spot, in the slightly warmed up oven for example.

Take the dough out of the oven and remove the cover.

Preheat the oven to 350°F (180°C) and place an ovenproof dish at the bottom filled with boiling water.

Lightly coat the brioche with melted vegan butter and place it in the oven when it reaches 250°F (125°C).

Bake for 22 to 25 minutes. If the brioche is browning too much, place a piece of aluminum foil on top.

Let it cool a few minutes and transfer to a cooling rack. Cover the brioche while it cools to prevent it from losing too much moisture.

Eat right away or cut into slices and freeze it to enjoy toasted any morning. Thaw in the microwave until warm and fluffy.

Potato Yeast

At times it can be tricky to find good active yeast, so I looked for alternatives or ways to use less. Turns out this yeast is the best find ever to make all things baking ultra-fluffy. Prepare the yeast 2 to 3 days in advance.

Makes	350 g
Prep time	30 min + 2h

250 g	**Potatoes**
80 g	**Cooking water**
17 g	**Sugar** (1 tbsp)
11 g	**Salt** (3 tsp)
¼ tsp	**Active dry yeast** (optional but will speed up the process)

Wash, peel, and roughly cut the potatoes, place in a saucepan and cover with water. Cook for 25 minutes or until tender (a knife should go through with no resistance). Keep the cooking water. Let it all cool in the pan for one hour.

Scoop the cooled potatoes into a large bowl. Add the cooking water, the sugar, the salt, and the yeast. Mix with an immersion blender until it is completely smooth. It will have the texture of stringy mashed potatoes. Transfer to a big jar, leaving enough room for it will double in size before sinking again. Cover with a cloth and let sit at room temperature for 48 to 72 hours. Then close the jar with a lid and store the potato yeast in the refrigerator.

This recipe can easily be doubled as it keeps for up to 2 months.

This potato yeast will not completely replace active dry yeast but will reduce the amount needed (about by half). In most recipes 10 grams of potato yeast for every 100 grams of flour is a good ratio but always add a little active dry yeast or the result will be too dense.

Use this potato yeast to make brioche, tigelle, challah, and more.

Tigelle

These are awesome little Italian breads that are baked in a pan or in a tigelle mold. No oven needed. Traditional Modena street food, they are crispy on the outside and fluffy on the inside. They are perfect for breakfast or as an appetizer dipped in olive oil.

Prep time: 30 minutes, 1 hour to proof, 30 minutes to shape, 1 hour to rest, and 25 minutes to cook

Makes 10 to 12

150 ml	**Water**
150 ml	**Oat milk** (p. 14)
½ tsp	**Active dry yeast**
50 g	**Potato yeast** (p. 20)
25 g	**Olive oil**
500 g	**Flour**
8 g	**Salt**

Heat the water and oat milk until lukewarm. Whisk in the active dry yeast and the potato yeast, let sit for 10 minutes to activate. You can omit the potato yeast, in that case use 5 g of active dry yeast instead of half a teaspoon.

Pour the milk and yeast mixture in the bowl of a stand mixer*. Pass it through a fine sieve if there are any lumps left and press hard with the back of a spoon to get everything out. Add the olive oil, the flour, and the salt. Knead using the hook of the stand mixer 5 minutes or until the dough comes together and forms a smooth ball.

Leave the dough in the bowl. Using a spatula, bring the dough towards the center to form a ball and lightly coat it with olive oil. Cover with a lid or plastic wrap and leave to prove somewhere warm for one hour.

**This dough can be kneaded by hand but that will take longer.*

Place the dough on a lightly floured surface and roll it out to a little more than half an inch thick (1½ cm). Using a round cookie cutter, cut out 10 to 12 neat discs of 3.5 inches (9 cm).

Place them on a silicon mat covered with flour or on a floured countertop. Cover with a cloth and leave to rest for 1 hour.

Heat a flat skillet or pan (no oil needed). Carefully take the tigelle from the silicon mat and cook in batches on medium to high heat until they are golden brown. Flip to cook the other side, about 4 minutes each side.

Eat right away or let cool covered with a cloth to preserve the moisture and freeze. Thaw in the microwave until warm and fluffy and toast them whole or cut them in half by poking them with a fork all the way around to optimize the toasting surface. This is called the fork-split method.

Enjoy for breakfast, use for sandwiches, grilled cheese or as an appetizer dipped in olive oil and herbs.

Chia Pudding

Chia seeds are a great way to get fiber, protein, and a little omega 3 in the morning. Very neutral in taste, this pudding can be topped with everything. Here are three variations.

Makes	1 portion
Prep time	10+30 min or overnight

150 ml	**Plant milk***
25 g	**Chia seeds**
2 tsp	**Maple syrup**
¼ tsp	**Vanilla extract**

Directly in a mason jar or in a bowl, combine all the ingredients and whisk thoroughly making sure there are no chia seed lumps. Let sit and stir again after 2 to 3 minutes to make sure the chia seeds are evenly distributed. Close the jar or cover the bowl and place in the refrigerator at least 30 minutes or overnight.

Add any topping you like.

For a summer chia bowl, top it with strawberries, peaches, raspberries, and maple syrup.

For autumn chia bowls, top it with:

- grilled pears, cashew butter, homemade granola**, and maple syrup;

- grilled plums, cinnamon, cashew butter, salted cashews, and maple syrup

The contrast between the cold chia pudding and the warm fruit is delicious. This is a great way to use overripe fruits.

*See recipes for homemade cashew milk p. 12 and for homemade oat milk p. 14.

** See recipe p. 34.

Challah

This challah is perfect. The texture is the right density, it has the ideal amount of sweetness to be enjoyed either for breakfast or with a main course. The oat milk and the potato yeast give it that extra fluffiness and buttery flavor.

Prep time: 30 minutes, 3 hours or overnight in the refrigerator to proof, 30 minutes to shape, 1 hour to rise, and 20 minutes to bake

Makes   15

295 ml	**Oat milk** (p. 14)
½ tsp	**Active dry yeast**
50 g	**Potato yeast** (p. 20)
30 ml	**Olive oil**
40 g	**Pumpkin puree**
490 g	**Flour**
50 g	**Sugar**
1 tsp	**Salt**

Glaze

| 15 ml | **Maple syrup** |
| 15 g | **Oat milk** |

Heat the oat milk to lukewarm, about 30 seconds in the microwave. Whisk in the active dry yeast and the potato yeast. Let sit for 10 minutes to activate.

Prepare the dry ingredients: flour, sugar, and salt. Roughly combine and set aside.

Pour the milk and yeast mixture in the bowl of a stand mixer*. Pass it through a fine sieve if there are any lumps left and press hard with the back of a spoon to get everything out. Add the olive oil and pumpkin puree, then the dry ingredients and knead for 5 minutes. Stop halfway to scrap down the sides. The dough should come together and form a smooth ball.

Using a spatula, bring the dough towards the center to form a ball. Transfer it to a bowl with enough room for it to rise and cover with a lid or plastic wrap. Chill in the refrigerator at least 3 hours or, even better, overnight (up to 24h) to enhance the flavor.

*The challah can be kneaded by hand but that will take longer.

Take the dough out of the refrigerator. Make either a 3 or 4 strand bread. For the latter, separate the dough into 4 equal parts. On a lightly floured surface roll each one out into a long log. Pinch the 4 together at the top and braid. You can find many videos to explain this, the easiest method is the one using a 2 number system (2 over, one in the middle). There are other methods, using 4 letters or 4 numbers, but they are more complicated.

Place the braid on a lined baking tray. Cover with plastic wrap and place 1 hour, or until it has doubled in size, in a warm spot like a slightly warmed up oven for example.

Take it out of the oven and remove the cover.

Preheat the oven to 350°F (180°C) and place an ovenproof dish at the bottom filled with boiling water.

Glaze the challah and place it in the oven when it reaches 250°F (125°C).

Bake for 20 to 25 minutes. If it browns too much, place a piece of aluminum foil on top.

Glaze a second time right out of the oven and transfer to a cooling rack. Cover the challah with a plastic cover while it cools to prevent it from drying.

Eat right away or cut into large slices and freeze to enjoy toasted anytime. Thaw in the microwave until warm and fluffy.

Chunky Cashew Granola

This recipe is very simple and keeps for at least a month. Crispy, not too sweet, it is perfect with homemade plant milk and fruit or to add some crunch to a yogurt.

| Makes | 765 g |
| Prep time | 40 min |

125 g	**Cashews**
480 g	**Quick oats**
½ tsp	**Salt**
80 g	**Coconut oil** (refined)
80 g	**Maple syrup**
1 tsp	**Vanilla extract**

Preheat the oven to 150°C (300° F).

Roughly chop the cashews.

In a large bowl combine the oats, chopped cashews, and salt.

Melt the coconut oil, add the maple syrup and vanilla extract, and pour on the oats. Mix to coat everything evenly.

Pour the granola onto a lined baking tray. Spread it evenly and press it down a bit with a soft spatula.

Bake for 20 to 25 minutes or until lightly golden. Do not bake too long otherwise it will be a little bitter. Let cool completely on the baking tray to allow the granola to harden. Lift the granola off the tray with a flat spatula, this will already break it up a bit.

Handle with care to keep some big chunks when transferring it to an airtight container.

Pancakes

This title should have exclamation marks because these are the fluffiest pancakes ever and the ingredients are so simple. For thick pancakes make the batter the night before.

Makes	18
Prep time	1h30

300 g	**Flour**
25 g	**Sugar**
22 g	**Baking powder***
25 g	**Vegan butter**
350 ml	**Oat milk** (p. 14)
60 g	**Apple sauce**

In a large bowl, combine the dry ingredients: flour, sugar, and baking powder.

Melt the vegan butter 20 seconds in the microwave. Add the oat milk and the apple sauce to the melted butter.

Pour everything on the dry ingredients and whisk until well combined. If there are any lumps use an immersion blender to get rid of them. Let the batter rest for 20 minutes or pour into an airtight container and place in the refrigerator overnight for fluffier pancakes.

Cook in a flat pan with a little vegan butter. Use a small pitcher or measuring cup to pour the batter directly into the pan, it's less messy. For fluffier pancakes, cook them on medium to low heat and flip them before the bubbles on top start to pop so that the air gets trapped in the pancakes and makes them rise even more.

Eat them with vegan butter and maple syrup or with nut butter, maple syrup, and a pinch of sea salt. These pancakes are freezer friendly.

**1 big tbsp*

Cinnamon Buns

Best cinnamon buns ever. The texture is amazing, incredibly soft and fluffy. The potato yeast gives them a wonderful buttery flavor.

Prep time: 30 minutes, 3 hours or overnight in the refrigerator to proof, 30 minutes to shape, 1h30 to rise, and 25 minutes to bake

Makes   11 to 12

210 ml	**Oat milk** (p. 14)
1 tsp	**Active dry yeast**
50 g	**Potato yeast** (p. 20)
80 g	**Vegan butter**
430	**Flour**
90 g	**Sugar**
Pinch of	**Salt**
1 tbsp	**Brown sugar**

Filling

40 g	**Vegan butter**
3 tsp	**Cinnamon**

The dough can be kneaded by hand but that will take longer.

Heat the oat milk to lukewarm, about 30 seconds in the microwave. Whisk in the active dry yeast and the potato yeast. Let sit for 10 minutes to activate.

Melt the vegan butter 20 seconds in the microwave.

Measure the dry ingredients: flour, sugar, and salt. Roughly combine. Set aside.

Pour the milk and yeast mixture in the bowl of a stand mixer*. Pass it through a fine sieve if there are any lumps left and press hard with the back of a spoon to get everything out. Add the vegan butter then the dry ingredients and knead for 6 to 8 minutes with a stand mixer. Stop halfway to scrap down the sides if needed. The dough will not completely detach from the bowl to form a ball, that's fine, it just needs to be smooth.

Using a spatula, bring the dough towards the center to form a rough ball. Transfer it to a bowl with enough room for it to rise a little. Cover with a lid or plastic wrap. Chill in the refrigerator at least 3 hours or, even better, overnight (up to 24h) to enhance the flavor.

Prepare the cinnamon filling just before shaping the buns. Soften the vegan butter and add the cinnamon. Using a spatula mix until well combined. Set aside in a cool place.

Lightly butter and flour a 9-inch (24 cm) round cake pan and 4 large baking cups in a muffin tins.

Take the dough out of the refrigerator. On a lightly floured surface, roll it out into a rectangle of about 20x16-inch (50 by 40 cm). It should be a little less than half an inch (1 cm) thick. Spread the cinnamon filling evenly on the entire surface, then roll tightly from top to bottom into a long cylinder.

With a knife, cut into 11 to 12 pieces and place them in the cake pan leaving enough space between each bun for them to rise. Place the rest in the muffin tins to make individual buns. Cover with plastic wrap and place 1h30, or until it has doubled in size, in a warm spot such as a slightly warmed up oven for example.

When the buns have doubled in size, take them out of the oven, remove the cover and sprinkle with coarse sugar.

Preheat the oven to 350°F (180°C) and place an oven resistant bowl in the bottom filled with boiling water. Start baking the buns when the oven reaches 250°F (125°C).

Bake for 22 to 25 minutes. If the buns are browning too much place a piece of aluminum foil on top. Let cool a couple of minutes.

Transfer to a cooling rack. Cover the buns with a plastic wrap while they cool to prevent them from losing too much moisture.

Eat right away or freeze in individual portions. Thaw in the microwave until warm and fluffy.

Orange Scones

These are more scone-inspired than scones, but they are delicious nonetheless. This recipe uses the oat pulp leftover from making homemade oat milk. They are very easy and quick to make. Enjoy them warm or freeze them for another day.

Makes	6	
Prep time	30 min	

60 g	**Coconut oil**
20 g	(refined)
45 g	**Vegan butter**
Zest of	**Sugar**
2 tbsp	**One orange**
60 ml	**Orange juice**
100 g	**Oat milk** (p. 14)
250 g	**Oat pulp***
1 tsp	**Flour**
A pinch	**Baking powder**
	Of salt

The oat milk and oat pulp need to be at room temperature otherwise the coconut oil will solidify.

Preheat the oven to 200°C (400°F).

Soften the coconut oil and the vegan butter. Beat them with the sugar and the orange zest. Add the orange juice, oat milk, oat pulp, and quickly combine. Then add the flour with the baking powder and salt. Stir until well combined but do not overmix or the oat pulp will make the dough gelatinous.

Scope the batter in a buttered and lightly floured small muffin tin.

Bake for 20 minutes.

Enjoy warm with vegan butter and jam.

*The amount leftover from the recipe for homemade oat milk p. 14.

English Muffins

A recipe book about breakfast wouldn't be complete without an English muffin recipe. These are perfectly fluffy and very easy to make. To optimize the toasting surface, cut the muffins in half using the fork-split method by poking it with a fork all the way around. This creates the traditional English muffins nooks and crannies.

Prep time: 30 minutes, 1 hour to proof, 30 minutes to shape, 40 minutes to rise, and 25 minutes to cook

Makes 9 to 10

270 ml	**Oat milk** (p. 14)
½ tsp	**Active dry yeast**
50 g	**Potato yeast** (p. 20)
50 g	**Vegan butter**
500 g	**Flour**
3 tsp	**Sugar**
1½ tsp	**Baking powder**
1 tsp	**Salt**
Optional	**Cornmeal**

Heat the oat milk to lukewarm, about 30 seconds in the microwave. Whisk in the active dry yeast and the potato yeast. Let sit for 10 minutes to activate. If not using potato yeast, use 2 tsp of active dry yeast instead of one.

Melt the vegan butter 20 seconds in the microwave and set aside.

Prepare the flour, sugar, baking powder, and salt. Roughly combine and set aside.

Pour the milk and yeast mixture in the bowl of a stand mixer*. Pass it through a fine sieve if there are any lumps left and press hard with the back of a spoon to get everything out. Add the vegan butter and the dry ingredients. Knead using the hook of the stand mixer about 5 minutes or until it comes together and makes a smooth dough.

Leave it in the bowl. Using a spatula, bring the dough towards the center to form a ball. Cover with a lid or a plastic cover and leave to prove somewhere warm for one hour.

*This dough can be kneaded by hand but that will take longer.

On a floured surface roll out the dough to about half an inch thick (1½ cm). Using a round cookie cutter of about 3,5 inches (9 cm), cut out 9 to 10 muffins.

Cover a silicon mat with cornmeal and place the cut out muffins on top. Sprinkle the other side with more cormeal. Cover with plastic wrap and let to rise for 40 minutes.

This step is optional but will give the English muffins their specific look.

Heat a flat skillet or pan (no oil needed). Carefully take the English muffins from the silicon mat and cook in batches on medium heat until golden brown. Flip to cook the other side, reduce the heat and cover with a lid to allow the muffins to cook through, about 5 minutes on each side.

Enjoy right away or let cool and freeze. Thaw in the microwave until warm and fluffy.

Olive Oil Rolls

Soft bread made with olive oil is very popular in the South of France. Why? Well because it's traditional and delicious. The olive oil will give the rolls a wonderfully dense texture and a little taste of sunshine.

Prep time: 30 minutes, 3 hours or overnight in the refrigerator to proof, 30 minutes to shape, 1h30 to rise, and 25 minutes to bake

Makes   7 to 8

210 ml	**Oat milk** (p. 14)
1 tsp	**Active dry yeast**
50 g	**Potato yeast** (p. 20)
60 ml	**Olive oil**
430 g	**Flour**
90 g	**Sugar**
½ tsp	**Salt**

**This dough can be kneaded by hand but that will take longer.*

Heat the oat milk to lukewarm, about 30 seconds in the microwave. Whisk in the active dry yeast and the potato yeast. Let sit for 10 minutes to activate.

Measure the olive oil separately.

Prepare the dry ingredients: flour, sugar, and salt. Roughly combine and set aside.

Pour the milk and yeast mixture in the bowl of a stand mixer*. Pass it through a fine sieve if there are any lumps left and press hard with the back of a spoon to get everything out. Add the olive oil then the dry ingredients and knead for 6 to 8 minutes with a stand mixer, stopping halfway to scrap down the sides. The dough will not completely detach from the bowl to form a ball, that's fine, it just needs to be smooth.

Using a spatula, bring the dough towards the center to form a rough ball. Transfer it to a bowl with enough space for it to rise and cover with a lid or plastic wrap. Chill in the refrigerator at least 3 hours or, even better, overnight (up to 24h) to enhance the flavor.

Lightly butter and flour a 9-inch (24 cm) round cake pan.

Take the dough out of the refrigerator.

On a lightly floured surface roll it out to form a long cylinder, cut into 7 or 8 equal pieces. To form a ball with each of them, roughly bring the edges underneath, then place on an un-floured surface, place your hand on the dough and roll making little circles gently pushing the dough under with your thumb.

Place the rolls in the cake pan, leaving enough space between each roll for them to double in size. Cover with plastic wrap and place 1h30, or until it has doubled in size, in a warm spot such as a slightly warmed up oven.

Take the dough out of the oven and remove the cover.

Preheat the oven to 350°F (180°C) and place an oven proof dish at the bottom filled with boiling water.

Start baking when the oven reaches 250°F (125°C).

Bake for 22 to 25 minutes. If the rolls are browning too much, place a piece of aluminum foil on top.

Let them cool a few minutes and transfer to a cooling rack. Cover the rolls while they cool to prevent them from losing too much moisture.

Enjoy right away or freeze in individual portions. Thaw in the microwave until warm and fluffy.

DESSERTS COOKIES AND CAKES

Crêpes

Yes, crêpes! They are perfect, the texture is wonderful, contain no refined sugar, and no complicated ingredients.

| Makes | 16 small |
| Prep time | 1h |

250 g	**Flour**
4 tbsp	**Cornstarch**
420 g	**Oat milk** (p. 14)
60 g	**Vegan butter**
4 tsp	**Maple syrup**
1 tsp	**Vanilla extract**
¼ tsp	**Salt**
Coconut	**Oil for cooking** (refined)

Melt the vegan butter 20 seconds in the microwave.

In a large bowl, add the flour and the cornstarch and roughly combine. Add the oat milk, melted vegan butter, maple syrup, vanilla extract, and salt. Whisk until completely smooth or mix with an immersion blender. Cover and let it rest for 30 minutes or place it in an airtight container and leave overnight in the refrigerator.

Tip: pour the batter in a container with a handle and a spout such like a measuring cup to make it easier to pour into the pan.

To cook the crêpes, heat a flat frying pan on high heat, dab it with a little refined coconut oil using a paper towel. Pour the batter whilst turning the pan to evenly distribute a thin layer on the entire surface.

Reduce the heat to medium-high. Cook for 2 to 3 minutes or until the crêpe detaches easily from the pan, flip it, and cook the other side for 1 to 2 minutes or until slightly colored. Repeat with the rest of the batter.

Enjoy them warm. They can also be frozen and reheated.

Date Cookies

Perfectly crumbly with a soft date filling, these cookies are the perfect treat. The dates can easily be replaced with figures.

Makes	20 to 24
Prep time	1h30

190 g	**Flour**
½ tsp	**Baking powder**
25 g	**White sugar**
¼ tsp	**Salt**
105 g	**Coconut oil** (refined)
60 g	**Ice cold water**

Filling

2 tbsp	**Vegan butter**
240 g	**Unpitted dates**
½ tsp	**Orange zest**
1 ½ tbsp	**Orange juice**
½ tsp	**Cinnamon**

In the bowl of a stand mixer using the hook (or in a food processor using on/off pulses) add the flour, baking powder, sugar, and salt. Gradually add the solid coconut oil until it has a sand-like consistency.

Add the ice-cold water, then knead a bit (knead by hand if using a food processor). If the dough is too dry add a little water.

Divide the dough in two, either form 2 balls or roll it out into 2 rectangles a little less than half an inch thick (less than 1 cm) on parchment paper, cover, and refrigerate for 30 minutes.

To make the filling, melt the vegan butter 20 seconds in the microwave. Add all the ingredients to a small food processor and coarsely mix. Add a little orange juice if the mixture is too dry. Cover and place in the refrigerator until needed.

Take the dough out of the refrigerator 10 minutes before otherwise
it will crack when shaping the cookies.

Preheat the oven to 375°F(190°C).

If the dough was refrigerated in 2 balls, roll it out on a lightly
floured surface into 2 rectangles a little less than half an inch thick
(less than 1 cm).

Cut both rectangles in half lengthwise, place some filling all along
the middle, fold gently but tightly the dough over to close. Cut into
squares and place on a lined baking sheet. Repeat with the rest of
the dough and the filling.

Bake for 14 to 19 minutes.

Let them firm up a couple of minutes before transferring to a
cooling rack. Store for up to 4 days in an airtight container.

Raspberry Chip Cookies

If you gently crush frozen raspberries, they will separate into tiny ruby flecks which are gorgeous. So why not use them to replace chocolate chips with raspberry chips.

Makes   10 to 12

Prep time   40 min

100 g	**Coconut oil** (refined)
110 g	**White sugar**
20 g	**Brown sugar**
1 tsp	**Vanilla extract**
50 g	**Coconut milk**
70 g	**Apple sauce**
300 g	**Flour**
1 tsp	**Cornstarch**
1 tsp	**Baking soda**
½ tsp	**Salt**
40 g	**Frozen raspberries**

Bring the coconut milk and the apple sauce to room temperature to prevent the coconut oil from solidifying in the dough.

Preheat the oven to 350°F (180°C).

Beat the coconut oil with the sugars and vanilla extract. Beat in the coconut milk and the apple sauce. Add the flour, cornstarch, baking soda, and salt to the wet ingredients and stir until well combined. Do not overmix.

Take the frozen raspberries, do not thaw them. Gently crush them to separate the drupelets into lots of tiny flecks. Gently fold the frozen raspberry chips into the dough. Be careful not to burst them. This step is a little messy. The dough will harden because of the frozen raspberries.

Using a spoon or even better an ice-cream scoop take some dough, shape the cookies and place them on a silicon mat. To achieve thick cookies do not flatten them.

Bake for 15 minutes. Transfer to a cooling rack and store in an airtight container.

Vanilla Custard

This recipe for vanilla custard is surprisingly simple and does not require any unusual ingredients. It is truly creamy and a must have in any vegan baking toolkit. Make this custard a few hours ahead of time or the day before.

Makes	4
Prep time	10 min + overnight

50 g	**Coconut oil** (refined)
70 g	**Cashew butter***
¼ of a	**Vanilla bean**
1 tsp	**Vanilla extract**
350 ml	**Oat milk** (p. 14)
25 g	**Sugar**
14 g**	**Cornstarch**

In a large bowl, add the coconut oil, cashew butter, vanilla bean, and vanilla extract.

Pour the oat milk and sugar in a saucepan, whisk in the cornstarch, mix with an immersion blender to make sure it is well combined and that there are no lumps. Cook on medium heat about 3 to 5 minutes, whisking constantly until it thickens. Be careful as it will thicken quickly because of the oat milk.

Pour the hot milk over the rest and mix with an immersion blender until completely smooth.

Pour in individual bowls or in a large mason jar and place in the refrigerator for at least 6 hours or overnight for a firmer custard.

*Can be replaced with almond butter or sunflower seed butter

**One big tablespoon

Oat and Earl Grey Cake

When making homemade oat milk, instead of throwing the oat pulp away make this cake. It is crispy on the outside and fluffy on the inside. Just what a cake should be.

Makes 16

Prep time 1h15

120 g	**Coconut oil** (refined)
40 g	**Vegan butter**
130 g	**Sugar**
2 tbsp	**Earl Grey tea leaves**
120 g	**Apple sauce**
200 g	**Oat pulp***
220 g	**Flour**
1 tsp	**Baking soda**
1 tsp	**Baking powder**
A pinch	**of salt**

Preheat the oven to 350°F (180°C).

Bring all the ingredients to room temperature, if they are too cold the coconut oil will solidify and make lumps in the batter.

Beat the coconut oil, vegan butter, sugar, and grinded tea leaves until light and fluffy. Beat in the apple sauce and the oat pulp. Add the flour, baking soda, baking powder, and salt at the same time. Beat or stir in until just combined. Do not overmix as it will activate the gelatinous properties of the oat pulp.

Butter and flour a 8x8-inch (20 by 20 cm) square bake pan. Pour the batter and spread it evenly as it will not spread when baking. Sprinkle with sugar.

Bake for 35 to 40 minutes.

Cut into squares. They are great the next day kept in a mason jar or an airtight container. They also freeze very well.

*Double the amount leftover from the recipe for homemade oat milk p. 14.

Blueberry Pie

One of the great joys of summer is the abondance of fruit. Blueberries are of course among the best, bursting with flavor and goodness. With this versatile pie crust recipe, you can create delectable pies using not only blueberries but any other fruit.

Makes 14 to 16

Prep time 2h

100 g	**Vegan butter**
120 g	**Coconut oil** (refined)
130 g	**White sugar**
1 tsp	**Vanilla extract**
80 g	**Apple sauce**
400 g	**Flour**
¾ tsp	**Salt**
300 g	**Blueberries** (fresh or frozen)

Bring the apple sauce and the vegan butter to room temperature to prevent the coconut oil from making lumps in the dough.

Beat the softened vegan butter, solid coconut oil, sugar, and vanilla extract until light and creamy. Beat in the apple sauce. Add the flour and the salt, beat or stir in until just combined. Using a spatula, bring the dough together to form a rough ball, cover, and chill in the refrigerator at least 30 minutes. The dough may be kept overnight in the refrigerator, in which case take it out 30 minutes before using.

Wash the blueberries and let them dry.

Preheat the oven to 350°F (180°C).

Place a 9x6-inch (24 by 16 cm) bottomless stainless-steel baking square on a lined baking tray or use a pie dish with a removable bottom. With your hands, separate the dough into crumble like pieces and press them down to form the pie. Do the same for the sides.

Spread the blueberries evenly into the pie crust. Sprinkle with a little sugar.

Bake for 35 to 45 minutes or until the crust turns golden.

Zucchini Bread

Adding zucchini to cakes is a great way to add moisture without the need for extra butter or oil. The zucchini blends seamlessly into the batter, leaving no trace of its presence in terms of flavor. Instead, it will result in a moist and tender cake with the perfect texture.

Makes   1

Prep time   1h45

380 g	**Flour**
1 tsp	**Baking powder**
1 tsp	**Baking soda**
1 tsp	**Salt**
1 tsp	**Cinnamon**
160 g	**Coconut oil** (refined)
80 g	**Vegan butter**
150 g	**White sugar**
60 g	**Brown sugar**
120 g	**Apple sauce**
2 tsp	**Vanilla extract**
340 g	**Grated zucchini**

Icing (optional)

5 tbsp	**Icing sugar**
2 tsp	**Water**

Preheat the oven to 350°F (180°C).

Prepare the dry ingredients: flour, baking powder, baking soda, salt, and cinnamon. Roughly combine and set aside.

Melt the coconut oil and the vegan butter. Pour them in a large bowl and beat with the sugars. Beat in the apple sauce (at room temperature) and vanilla extract. Add the dry ingredients to the wet ingredients, beat or stir to combine.

Wash and thinly grate the zucchini. Squeeze to remove a little moisture, then gently fold them in using a spatula.

Butter and flour a 10x4-inch (26 by 11 cm) loaf pan. Pour the batter in and bake for 1h20. Halfway through, place a piece of aluminum foil on the cake to prevent it from browning too much.

Remove from the oven, transfer to a plate or cutting board, and let cool before icing. Cover the cake with plastic wrap while it cools to prevent it from losing too much moister.

This zucchini bread is perfect the next day or can be cut into large slices and frozen. Thaw overnight.

Raspberry Cream

This recipe came to be because I was looking for a way to use slightly overripe raspberries. They are so delicious and so precious, it's always heartbreaking when they are forgotten a little too long in the refrigerator. No more worries, next time this happens it will be the perfect excuse to make this dessert.

Makes	4
Prep time	25 min + 3h

200 g	**Raspberries**
80 g	**Cashew butter**
20 g	**Coconut oil** (refined)
A pinch	**of salt**
Optional	**Maple syrup**

This recipe calls for very, very smooth cashew butter. The smoothest there is. It should also work with smooth almond butter or sunflower butter.

Wash and place the raspberries in a saucepan, add a little water to prevent them from burning, cover, and cook for a few minutes. There should be no cooking water left. Let cool for 15 minutes.

Add all the ingredients and mix in a food processor until smooth, scraping down the sides as needed. Transfer to ramequins or small glasses for individual portions, cover, and refrigerate at least 3 hours.

They will keep for a couple of days.

Enjoy with fresh raspberries and a splash of maple syrup.

Pumpkin Cake

Adding vegetables to desserts is the perfect way to make them healthier, lighter, and fluffier. Pumpkin is no exception. This cake is super moist, a little dense to give it the perfect bite, and loaded with autumn flavors.

| Makes | 16 |
| Prep time | 1 h |

150 g	**Coconut oil** (refined)
150 g	**White sugar**
30 g	**Brown sugar**
150 g	**Pumpkin puree**
30 g	**Oat milk** (p. 14)
1 ½ tsp	**Vanilla extract**
3 tsp	**Cinnamon**
375 g	**Flour**
1 tsp	**Baking powder**
1 tsp	**Baking soda**
½ tsp	**Salt**

Bring the oat milk and pumpkin puree to room temperature, otherwise the coconut oil will solidify and make lumps in the batter.

Beat the softened coconut oil with the sugars until creamy. Add the pumpkin puree, oat milk, vanilla extract, and cinnamon. Beat to combine.

Add the flour, baking powder, baking soda, and salt. Beat or stir in. Do not overmix.

Cover and chill in the refrigerator the batter for 30 minutes to enhance the flavors.

Preheat the oven to 375°F(190°C).

Butter and flour a 8x8-inch (20 by 20 cm) cake pan. Pour the batter and spread it evenly as it will not spread when baking.

Bake for 35 to 40 minutes or until a knife tip comes out clean.

These pumpkin squares are great the next day and freeze perfectly.

Chocolate Covered Cookie Bites

They are seriously addictive. Crunchy and salty, you'll never eat just one. The fact that they are bite size does not help, it's way too easy to keep going back.

Makes   a lot

Prep time 1h30

75 g	**Coconut oil** (refined)
80 g	**Vegan butter**
90 g	**Sugar**
½ tsp	**Vanilla extract**
55 g	**Apple sauce**
300 g	**Flour**
¾ tsp	**Salt**

Coating

100 g	**Dark Chocolate**
20 g*	**Coconut Oil**
½ tsp	(refined)
Pinch of	**Vanilla extract**
	Sea salt

*2 tbsp

Bring the apple sauce and the vegan butter to room temperature to prevent the coconut oil from making lumps in the dough.

Beat the solid coconut oil, softened vegan butter, sugar, and vanilla extract until light and creamy. Quickly beat in the apple sauce. Add the flour and salt. Stir until well incorporated. Do not overmix. Cover the dough and chill in the refrigerator for 30 minutes to make it easier to work later. The dough can also be kept in the refrigerator overnight, in which case take it out 15 minutes before using.

Preheat the oven to 350°F (180°C).

Prepare a lined baking tray. Take big pieces of dough and break them apart into lots of bites size pieces a little bigger than a hazelnut. They do not need to have the same size or shape.

Bake for 13 to 15 minutes or until they are slightly golden. Turn them around on the tray if needed. Let cool a couple of minutes.

Melt the chocolate for one and a half minutes in the microwave until melted and smooth. Combine with the coconut oil and vanilla extract. Pour half of the chocolate and of the cookie bites in a large bowl. Gently stir with a spatula to coat evenly. Place them on a baking sheet, sprinkle with a little sea salt. Repeat with the rest of the cookie bites. Let them cool completely until the chocolate harden.

Store these cookies in the refrigerator otherwise the chocolate will melt.

Pear Tonka Bean Oat Cake

A quick and easy recipe and a great way to use overripe fruits. Tonka beans are small black wrinkled seeds which come from the Amazon. They have a strong taste of vanilla and almond extract. They are very flavorful, the quantity needed will depend on their size and quality. They can be replaced with vanilla beans.

Makes 10 to 12

Prep time 45 min

280 g	**Quick oats**
180 g	**Flour**
100 g	**White sugar**
20 g	**Brown sugar**
1 tsp	**Baking powder**
½ tsp	**Salt**
100 g	**Coconut oil** (refined)
100 g	**Vegan butter**
1 tsp	**Vanilla extract**
3	**Pears**
½ a	**Tonka Bean**

In a large bowl, add all the dry ingredients: oats, flour, white and brown sugar, baking powder, and salt. Roughly mix. Melt the the coconut oil and the vegan butter together in the microwave. Once melted add the vanilla extract. Pour over the dry ingredients and beat or stir in right away until everything is well coated.

Preheat the oven to 350°F (180°C).

Wash, peel and cut the pears into into thick slices.

Transfer a little more than half of the mixture to a baking tray with a removable bottom or to a stainless-steel bottomless baking square of 10x6-inch (26 by 16 cm). Press it down evenly, add the pears to cover the whole surface, grate some tonka bean on top using a fine grater (as you would for nutmeg). Add the remaining cake mixture over the pears and press down gently.

Bake for 30 minutes. Transfer to a cutting board and let it completely cool before cutting ortherwise the cake will crumble.

It keeps for up to four days in an airtight container and is freezer friendly.

Pumpkin Cookies

Crunchy on the outside and chewy on the inside, they are perfect. With a hint of cinnamon, these cookies make you feel like home.

Makes 12

Prep time 1h

55 g	**Vegan butter**
60 g	**Coconut oil** (refined)
50 g	**Blond sugar**
50 g	**Brown sugar**
1 tsp	**Vanilla extract**
80 g	**Pumpkin puree**
190 g	**Flour**
¼ tsp	**Baking soda**
¼ tsp	**Baking powder**
1 tsp	**Cinnamon**
½ tsp	**Salt**

Bring the pumpkin puree to room temperature.

In a large bowl, beat the softened vegan butter, coconut oil, sugars, and vanilla until light and creamy. Beat or stir in the pumpkin puree.

Add the flour, baking soda, baking powder, half the cinnamon, and salt. Beat or stir in until well combined. Do not overmix.

Cover and chill the dough in the refrigerator for 30 minutes.

Preheat the oven to 350°F (180°C).

With an ice cream scope take about 25 g of dough, roll into a ball. Repeat with the rest of the dough.

Add blond sugar and the other half of cinnamon to a small bowl, toss the dough balls to coat them evenly. Place them on a lined baking tray, lightly flatten the cookies for they will not spread when baking and bake for 10 to 12 minutes.

Transfer to a cooling rack and store in an airtight container for up to a week.

Apple Cinnamon Cake

This is the best apple cake ever. It is made with the oat pulp leftover from making homemade oat milk. It is moist, fluffy, and packed with cinnamon flavor.

Makes   16

Prep time   1 h

40 g	**Vegan butter**
120 g	**Coconut oil** (refined)
130 g	**Sugar**
2 tsp	**Cinnamon**
120 g	**Apple sauce**
200 g	**Oat pulp***
220 g	**Flour**
1 tsp	**Baking soda**
1 tsp	**Baking powder**
A pinch	**of salt**
2	**Small apples**

Bring all the ingredients to room temperature to prevent the coconut oil from hardening and making lumps in the batter.

Preheat the oven to 350°F (180°C).

Beat the softened vegan butter, coconut oil, sugar, and cinnamon until light and creamy. Beat in the apple sauce and the oat pulp. Add the flour, baking soda, baking powder, and salt. Stir until just combined. Do not over mix as the oat pulp can make it a little gelatinous.

Wash and peel the apples. Cut them into small squares. Gently fold them in with a spatula.

Butter and flour a 8x8-inch (20 by 20 cm) cake pan. Pour the batter and spread it evenly as it will not spread when baking.

Mix 1 tbsp of brown sugar with a little cinnamon and sprinkle over the cake before baking.

Bake for 35 to 40 minutes.

Cut into squares. It is great the next day kept in an airtight container. It also freezes very well.

*Double the amount leftover from the recipe for homemade oat milk p. 14.

Flourless Nut Butter Cookies

Yes, flourless chocolate chip cookies. At first it is hard to believe it is possible to make cookies without any flour, but this recipe really works. It can be made with different nut butters, so don't hesitate to swap them according to your preferences.

Makes	12
Prep time	40 min

12 g	**Chia seeds**
40 g	**Water**
150 g	**Peanut butter**
100 g	**Cashew butter**
60 g	**Brown sugar**
¾ tsp	**Baking soda**
½ tsp	**Vanilla extract**
¼ tsp	**Salt**
50 g	**Chocolate chips**

To make the chia "egg", grind the chia seeds in a small food processor into a powder. Add the water, stir thoroughly, and let set for 15 minutes.

Preheat the oven to 350°F (180°C).

Beat the nut butters with the chia "egg". Heat the nut butters up a little before if they are too hard. Beat or stir in the sugar, baking soda, vanilla extract, and salt. Using a spatula, fold in the chocolate chips.

Form 12 balls and place them on a silicon mat or baking paper. Flatten slightly and bake for 12 to 14 minutes.

Add a few chocolate chips for looks right out of the oven.

Let cool and transfer to a rack. Store in an airtight container. They keep for several days.

Earl Grey Cookies

These cookies have a delightful crumbly texture, a perfect balance of sweetness, and are infused with the unique and aromatic flavor of Earl Grey tea. They are made using simple ingredients that enhance the overall taste.

Makes	24
Prep time	1h30

120 g	**Coconut oil** (refined)
100 g	**Vegan butter**
130 g	**Sugar**
½ tsp	**Vanilla extract**
2 tbsp	**Earl Grey tea leaves**
80 g	**Apple sauce**
400 g	**Flour**
1 tsp	**Salt**

Bring the apple sauce to room temperature otherwise the coconut oil will solidify and make lumps in the dough or melt if the apple sauce is too warm.

Beat the solid coconut oil, softened vegan butter, sugar, vanilla extract, and tea leaves until light and creamy.

Quickly beat in the apple sauce. Add the flour and the salt. Stir until incorporated. Do not overmix. Place the dough in a bowl, bring it together to form a rough ball, cover, and chill in the refrigerator for 30 minutes to make it easier to work. The dough can be kept in the refrigerator overnight, in which case take it out 15 minutes before shaping the cookies.

Preheat the oven to 350°F (180°C).

On a lightly flowered surface roll out the dough to less than half an inch thick (less than 1 cm), cut out using any cookie cutter. These are a little over 2 inches (6,5 cm). Repeat with the rest of the dough. Place them on a silicon mat or a lined baking tray, sprinkle with a little sugar, and bake for 18 to 20 minutes or until the edges are slightly golden.

Transfer to a cooling rack and let them cool before storing in an airtight container.

These cookies keep perfectly for at least a week.

Lemon Poppy Seed Cookies

This classic combination of flavors truly shines in a cookie. These treats are a perfect balance of sweetness and tanginess, topped with a crumbly texture.

Makes   24

Prep time   1h30

120 g	**Coconut oil** (refined)
100 g	**Vegan butter**
130 g	**Sugar**
½ tsp	**Vanilla extract**
Zest of	**One Lemon**
4 tbsp	**Lemon juice**
80 g	**Apple sauce**
400 g	**Flour**
1 tbsp	**Poppy seeds**
1 tsp	**Salt**

Icing

100 g	**Icing sugar**
4 tsp	**Lemon juice**

Bring the apple sauce to room temperature, too cold the coconut oil will solidify and make lumps in the dough, too warm it will melt.

Beat the solid coconut oil, softened vegan butter, sugar, vanilla, lemon zest, and lemon juice until light and creamy.

Quickly beat in the apple sauce. Add the flour, poppy seeds, and salt. Stir until just incorporated. Do not overmix. Place the dough in a bowl, bring together to form a rough ball, cover, and chill in the refrigerator for 30 minutes to make it easier to work. The dough can also be kept in the refrigerator overnight, in which case take it out 15 minutes before shaping the cookies.

Preheat the oven to 350°F (180°C).

On a lightly flowered surface, roll out the dough to a little less than half an inch thick (less than 1 cm), cut out using any shape of cookie cutter. Place them on a silicon mat or a lined baking tray. Bake for 18 to 20 minutes or until the edges are slightly golden.
Transfer to a cooling rack and let them cool before icing.

For the icing, thoroughly mix the lemon juice and the icing sugar until you have the desired relatively thick consistency. Ice the cookies and let the icing harden before storing in an airtight container.

These cookies keep perfectly for up to a week.

Chocolate Cake

A book about desserts wouldn't be complete without a chocolate cake recipe. This one has no unusual ingredients and is perfectly moist. The icing makes it the decadent dessert it should be.

Makes   24

Prep time 1h to 1h30

240 ml	**Oat milk** (p. 14)
1 tbsp	**Lemon juice**
50 ml	**Expresso**
60 g	**Coconut oil** (refined)
150 g	**Sugar**
2 tsp	**Vanilla extract**
80 ml	**Water** (lukewarm)
120 g	**Apple sauce**
240 g	**Flour**
120 g	**Cacao powder**
1 tbsp	**Baking powder**
1 tsp	**Baking soda**
1 tsp	**Salt**

Frosting

50 g	**Coconut oil** (refined)
100 g	**Maple syrup**
100 g	**Cashew butter**
2 tsp	**Vanilla extract**
50 g	**Cacao powder**
½ tsp	**Sea salt**

Mix the oat milk and the lemon juice. Let it rest for 10 minutes. Make the expresso, let it cool. Melt the coconut oil 30 seconds in the microwave.

Preheat the oven to 350°F (180°C).

In a large bowl mix the melted coconut oil with the sugar and the vanilla extract. Add the oat milk, expresso, water, and apple sauce. Whisk until well combined.

Measure the flour, cacao powder, baking powder, baking soda, and salt. Roughly combine. Add them to the wet ingredients and mix until there are no dry ingredients visible. Do not overmix.

Pour the batter in either two 8-inch (20 cm) buttered and lightly floured baking pans or buttered and lightly floured muffin tins.

Bake for 40 to 45 minutes for the big cakes or for 28 minutes for the muffin size. Transfer to a cooling rack.

For the frosting, melt the coconut oil, add the maple syrup. With a spatula, combine with creamy cashew butter, vanilla, and salt. When well combined, stir in the cacao powder.

Let the cakes completely cool before icing.

Vanilla Christmas Cookies

These are the perfect cookies to decorate any way you like. And the Holidays are always a very good excuse to make more cookies.

Makes 24

Prep time 1h30

120 g	**Coconut oil** (refined)
100 g	**Vegan butter**
130 g	**Sugar**
½ tsp	**Vanilla extract**
½	**Vanilla bean**
80 g	**Apple sauce**
400 g	**Flour**
1 tsp	**Salt**

Icing

50 g	**Icing sugar**
2 tsp	**Water**

Bring the apple sauce to room temperature, too cold the coconut oil will solidify and make lumps in the dough, too warm it will melt.

Beat the solid coconut oil, softened vegan butter, sugar, vanilla, and the seeds from the vanilla bean until light and creamy.

Quickly beat in the apple sauce. Add the flour, and salt. Stir until just evenly incorporated. Place the dough in a bowl, bring it together to form a rough ball, cover, and chill in the refrigerator for 30 minutes to make it easier to work. The dough can be kept in the refrigerator overnight, in which case take it out 15 minutes before shaping the cookies.

Preheat the oven to 350°F (180°C).

On a lightly flowered surface, roll out the dough to a little less than hthick, cut out using any shape of cookie cutter. Place them on a silicon mat or a lined baking tray. Bake for 18 to 20 minutes or until the edges are slightly golden.

Transfer to a cooling rack and let them cool before icing.

For the icing, combine the water and icing sugar until you have the desired thick consistency. Ice the cookies and let the icing harden before storing in an airtight container.

These cookies keep perfectly for up to a week.

 On a Vegan Table *When delicious happens to be Vegan*

Tonka Bean Crescents

Tonka beans have a very distinctive flavor of almond and vanilla with a hint of caramel. If you can't find tonka beans replace them with vanilla beans.

Makes	50
Prep time	1h30

120 g	**Coconut oil** (refined)
100 g	**Vegan butter**
130 g	**Sugar**
½ tsp	**Vanilla extract**
½ to 1	**Tonka bean**
80 g	**Apple sauce**
400 g	**Flour**
1 tsp	**Salt**
10 g	**Icing sugar**

Bring the apple sauce to room temperature, too cold the coconut oil will solidify and make lumps in the dough, too warm it will melt.

Beat the solid coconut oil, softened vegan butter, sugar, the vanilla extract, and the grated tonka bean until light and creamy. Grate the tonka bean with a very fine grater, the kind that is used for nutmeg.

Quickly beat in the apple sauce. Add the flour and salt. Stir until just incorporated. Place the dough in a bowl, bring it together to form a rough ball, cover, and chill in the refrigerator for 30 minutes to make it easier to work. The dough can also be kept in the refrigerator overnight, in which case take it out 15 minutes before shaping the cookies.

Preheat the oven to 350°F (180°C).

Take a small tablespoon of cookie dough of about 16 g, roll into a ball, then into a cylinder and round it into a crescent shape pinching the ends. Repeat with the rest of the dough.
Place the cookies on a silicon mat, or a lined baking tray and bake for 18 to 20 minutes or until the edges are slightly golden.

Transfer to a cooling rack, dust with icing sugar while they are still a little warm. Transfer to an airtight container. These cookies keep perfectly for at least a week.

On a Vegan Table *When delicious happens to be Vegan*

CONVERSION CHART

Ingredients	Grams	US Cups
Apple sauce	125 g	1/2
Brown sugar	200 g	1
Cacao powder	100 g	1
Coconut oil	200 g	1
Flour	125 g	1
Icing sugar	125 g	1
Nut butter	250 g	1
Oats	100 g	1
Plant milk	240 ml	1
Vegan butter	200 g	1
Pumpkin puree	100 g	1/2
White sugar	200 g	1

NB: 1 ml of liquid = 1 g